Children in our World

Rights and Equality

Marie Murray

Hanane Kai

NEWHAM LIBRARIES

First published in Great Britain in 2020 by Wayland

Text © Hodder and Stoughton, 2020
Illustrations © Hanane Kai, 2020

The rights of Hanane Kai to be identified as the illustrator of the Work has been asserted by her in accordance with the Copyright, Designs and Patents Act 1988.

Edited by Sarah Peutrill
Designed by Hanane Kai
Hand texturing of illustrations by Mariela Gallegos

ISBN (HB): 978 1 5263 1099 6
ISBN (PB): 978 1 5263 1100 9

Printed and bound in China

Wayland, an imprint of
Hachette Children's Group
Part of Hodder and Stoughton
Carmelite House
50 Victoria Embankment
London EC4Y 0DZ
An Hachette UK Company
www.hachette.co.uk
www.hachettechildrens.co.uk

MIX
Paper from
responsible sources
FSC® C104740
FSC
www.fsc.org

The website addresses (URLs) included in this book were valid at the time of going to press. However, it is possible that contents or addresses may have changed since the publication of this book. No responsibility for any such changes can be accepted by either the author or the Publisher.

Contents

There are things we all need to be able to live well and safely. These are called rights.

All people have equal value, and this means that all of us have equal rights. It doesn't matter if we are young or old, sick or healthy, or poor or rich. It doesn't matter where we are born, what colour our skin is or what we believe.

There may be things that you want, like a trip to the zoo or a new toy. But these are different from the things that you need. So, how can we know the difference and decide what our rights are? How do we make sure that all the people in the world are treated equally and have what they need?

In 1948, a group of people from many different countries agreed on a list of rights that all people should have. This list is called the Universal Declaration of Human Rights. Since it was created a long time ago, we can keep adding to it, but it is a good place to start when we talk about human rights.

The first of these human rights is the right to be alive and be safe. This is called the right to life. It's the starting point for all human rights.

Work is a very important part of life. People need to be able to work so that they have the money to buy what they need – and even some things that they want – and to take care of their families. Along with the right to work comes the right to rest, recover and enjoy life.

Everyone has the right to be a free person and not be held in slavery. There are different kinds of slavery, but slaves are usually forced to work very hard for little or no pay.

All people deserve the chance to live a healthy life. They have the right to food, clothing and a place to live. They should be able to see a doctor when they are sick. They should get help if they lose their jobs or if they are too sick or elderly to care for themselves.

You might love going to school, or sometimes think you'd rather not go! But how would you feel if you couldn't ever go to school? All children have the right to go to school and get a good education, so they can succeed in life.

Everyone has the right to get married if they want to, and have a family. No one should be forced to get married if they don't want to or if they are too young.

Everyone has the right to their own beliefs and opinions, as long as their beliefs do not cause them to harm others. They can be part of whatever religion they choose, or no religion, and they have the right to leave a religion if they want to. Different beliefs and opinions help people to learn from each other and see other points of view.

Everyone deserves to be protected by just laws, and have a fair trial in a court. Before anyone is put in prison, a trial means they can stand in front of a judge and sometimes a jury. The judge and jury listen to the story and look at evidence to decide if the person is innocent or guilty.

Even in prison, people have rights. All forms of torture go against human rights. Even if people have done something very bad, they should not be tortured.

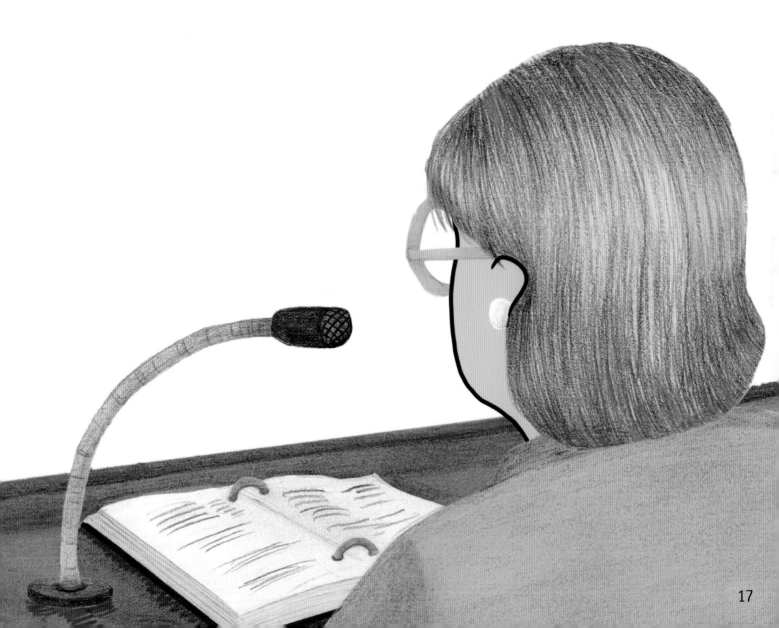

If good laws do not protect people in their own country, they have the right to leave and go anywhere they can so that they can be safe. When people are in danger, they have the right to move to a new place and seek safety.

Sometimes, other countries do not want to welcome people who are trying to escape danger. Governments might ignore the human rights of these people and say that people from certain countries are not welcome.

Sadly, although we should all have these human rights, the world is not fair and equal yet. Not everyone has the things they need, including safety, homes and food.

People live in war zones, refugee camps or places where there isn't enough food. Sometimes parents don't have enough money to send their children to school. Some countries have governments that are not fair. They may imprison or torture people that stand against them.

In places where not everyone has their rights respected, some people fight for equality. They are called human rights activists. People may choose to go on protest marches. Others choose to call or write to members of government and tell them when they see groups of people being treated poorly. Some become politicians themselves and try to fight for change.

Children have rights just as adults do. They have the right to food, a home and care. They also have the right to play. Parents share responsibility for bringing up children and should do what is best for them.

Governments should help parents care for their children by offering things like free schooling, healthcare or money for housing when families need it.

Every single person can do things to make
sure that those around them are treated with
equality and respect.

Sometimes people are bullied because they are different, or maybe for no reason at all. Often, bullies do not realise how much they are hurting another person. Defending a classmate or child who is being bullied, and asking the bully to stop, is a brave way to fight for equality and to inspire others to do the same.

Equality

Freedom

It isn't always easy to stand up for human rights and equality, but it is the right thing to do. There will probably be times when you are not treated well, and you will want someone to stand up for you, too.

Every day, people are working to make sure everyone's rights are protected. What are small or big ways that you can fight for equality?

Find Out More

Books

We're All Equal (I'm a Global Citizen)
Georgia Amson-Bradshaw & David Broadbent, Franklin Watts, 2019

We Are All Born Free: The Universal Declaration of Human Rights in Pictures
Amnesty International, Lincoln Children's Books, 2015

Dreams of Freedom
Amnesty International, Lincoln Children's Books, 2015

Websites

Amnesty International is the leading charity that works to protect people's human rights.
www.amnesty.org.uk

Save the Children is a charity that fights for children's rights.
www.savethechildren.org.uk

Video clip describing young people's rights under international human rights law in friendly language.
http://tinyurl.com/jv66q6v

Glossary

beliefs ideas or values that people accept to be true

bullying trying to harm or intimidate someone

equal having the same value

government the body of people who lead a country

judge an official who decides cases in a court

jury a group of people who look at evidence in court to decide whether someone is innocent or guilty

opinions views or ways of thinking that may not always be based on facts

politicians people who are chosen to be part of a government

prison a place where people are held when they have committed a crime or broken a law

refugee camps temporary places where people stay when they are escaping war or hardship in their country

religion a group of members who share beliefs and often gather to worship

respect to treat someone or something with dignity

responsibility having a duty to deal with something or of having control over someone

rights the things that people need and should have to live well and safely

slavery the practice of treating a person as property and forcing them to work for little or no pay

torture to cause deliberate harm to another person

Index